Simple Pantry & Refrigerator Leftover Reuse Recipes

Straight-Cut and Smart Ways to Practice Zero-Waste at Home

BY: Martin Beasant

Notification Page

Hello there,

I kindly request that you refrain from reproducing this book in any form, whether it be printed or electronic, sold, published, disseminated or distributed without obtaining prior written permission from the author.

I have taken great care in ensuring that the content of this book is accurate and helpful, but it is the reader's responsibility to exercise caution in their actions. Please note that the author cannot be held responsible for any consequences resulting from the reader's actions.

Thank you for your understanding and cooperation.

Sincerely,

Martin Beasant

●˙●．●˙●．●˙●．●˙●．●˙●．●˙●．●˙●．●˙●．●˙●．

Table of Contents

Introduction

Visualize a kitchen where nothing goes to waste! Every ingredient is treasured and used wisely and maximally for sustainability.

Leftovers from the previous days are transformed into delectable meals. Old pantry staples get revamps in creative, fun, and delicious eats and drinks. And when there are food scraps, they get made into meals and are finally tossed into compost for gardening. Zero-waste at it! (Do check out our cookbook for using food scraps sumptuously.)

It is a feeling of bliss knowing that you save cost, use resources wisely, and contribute to keeping the planet safe.

This cookbook is all about that; sharing thirty simple and smart ways to forage fridge leftovers and old pantry staples for tasty dishes.

So, the next time you've got leftovers of any sort, stay calm as a delicious way to reuse them is just right up your alley.

Pantry Leftovers

1. Mixed Seasoning

Make a blend of old spices and herbs for a new seasoning addition to your pantry.

Prep Time: 10 mins

Ingredients:

- Remaining bits of dried herbs, spices, and seasonings

Instructions:

1. Mix and match herbs, spices, and seasonings. Combine as desired and store in an airtight container.
2. Use for your desired recipes.

2. Vegetarian Meatballs

Use stale bread to create vegetarian nut-based meatballs. You can also soak the stale bread in milk for making meaty meatballs.

Prep Time: 20 mins

Cook Time: 6 mins

Serves: 7 to 8

Ingredients:

- ⅔ cup stale bread
- ¼ cup walnuts, finely chopped
- 1 large egg or ¼ cup aquafaba
- 2 tbsp grated Parmesan or plant-based cheese
- 2 sprigs fresh basil, stalks and leaves finely chopped
- Kosher salt and black pepper to taste
- 2 tbsp extra-virgin olive oil

Instructions:

1. Add the bread, walnuts, egg or aquafaba, cheese, basil, salt, and black pepper. Mix until well combined. Form 7 to 8 balls from the mixture.
2. Heat the olive oil in a nonstick skillet over medium heat. Fry the meatballs for 1 to 3 minutes per side or until golden brown. Drain on paper towels and serve as desired.

3. Bean Soup

Enjoy a rich bean soup made from the remainder of canned beans in your pantry. A mixture of bean colors is beautiful if you have bits of different ones.

Prep Time: 10 mins

Cook Time: 45 mins

Serves: 8

Ingredients:

- 2 tsp vegetable oil
- 2 medium onions, roughly chopped
- 3 large carrots, cut into ½-inch cubes
- 2 cups coarsely chopped celery
- 3 medium garlic cloves, finely minced
- 2 (15 oz) cans chopped tomatoes
- 2 cups assorted canned beans, drained and rinsed
- 1 cup diced smoked ham, optional
- 2 cups vegetable stock or water
- Chili pepper flakes to taste
- 1 tbsp balsamic vinegar
- Kosher salt and black pepper to taste
- Chopped fresh parsley

Instructions:

1. Heat the oil in a large pot over medium heat. Sauté the onions, carrots, and celery for 5 minutes. Stir in the garlic and cook for 1 minute or until fragrant.
2. Add the tomatoes, beans, ham, vegetable stock, chili pepper flakes, and balsamic vinegar. Cover, bring to a boil, and then simmer for 30 to 45 minutes or until the beans are well-warmed through.
3. Season with salt and black pepper. Stir the parsley through and serve warm.

4. Banana and Cereal Sushi

Before leftover cereal flattens out, transform it into these kid-friendly sushi-like snacks.

Prep Time: 20 mins

Serves: 12

Ingredients:

- 2 large bananas, quantity dependent on how much cereal you have
- 2 tbsp creamy nut or seed butter of choice
- 2 cups leftover cereal

Instructions:

1. Peel the bananas and slice onto 2-inch rounds.
2. Pour the nut or seed butter on a plate and the cereal on another plate.
3. Roll the sides of each banana in nut or seed butter, then roll it in the cereal, slightly pressing to adhere.
4. Arrange the banana sushi on a clean plate and serve.

5. All-In-One Soup

Make a rustic combo of canned vegetables and canned soups, even canned meats nearing their expiry dates into a delicious warm soup.

Prep Time: 15 mins

Cook Time: 36 mins

Serves: 4

Ingredients:

- 2 tbsp olive oil, divided
- 1 lb. beef stew meat
- Kosher salt and black pepper to taste
- 2 medium onions, roughly chopped
- 3 large carrots, cut into ½-inch cubes
- 2 cups coarsely chopped celery
- 3 medium garlic cloves, finely minced
- 2 (15 oz) cans soup of choice
- 1 cup beef or vegetable stock or water
- Other seasonings to taste, as preferred, optional
- Chopped fresh parsley

Instructions:

1. Heat 1 tbsp of olive oil in a large pot over medium heat. Next, season the meat with salt and black pepper. Brown the meat in the pot for 4 to 5 minutes. Remove the meat onto a plate.
2. Heat the remaining olive oil in the pot and sauté the onions, carrots, and celery for 5 minutes. Stir in the garlic and cook for 1 minute or until fragrant.
3. Stir in the beef, soup, and stock. Cover, bring to a boil, and then simmer for 20 to 25 minutes or until heated through. Adjust the taste with salt and black pepper.
4. Serve the soup garnished with parsley.

6. Granola

Easily use stale oats for granola and add whatever leftovers of nuts, dried fruits, seeds, and chocolate chips that you have.

Prep Time: 15 mins

Cook Time: 30 mins

Serves: 4 to 6

Ingredients:

- 2 cups stale oats
- ½ cup leftover nuts and seeds
- ½ cup coconut flakes, optional
- 2 tsp cinnamon
- ½ tsp sea salt
- ¼ cup maple syrup
- 2 tbsp melted coconut oil
- 2 tbsp creamy almond butter
- ⅓ cup leftover dried fruits, optional
- ⅓ cup leftover chocolate chips

Instructions:

1. Preheat the oven to 300°F.
2. Mix the oats, nuts, and seeds, coconut flakes, cinnamon, and salt in a bowl. Add the maple syrup, coconut oil, and almond butter. Mix well.
3. Spread the mixture on a baking sheet and press into a 1-inch thick round to encourage clumping. Bake for 15 minutes, turning the baking sheet halfway through cooking. Use a fork to break up the granola a little bit and bake for 15 more minutes or until golden brown.
4. Let cool completely and mix with the dried fruits and chocolate chips, if using. Store in an airtight container.

7. Pancake Mix

Say bye to boxed pancake mixes and make one yourself. Combine leftovers of baking supplies like flour, baking powder, cocoa powder, sugar, etc. You can always remake your pancake mix even from new baking supplies. It's that easy!

Prep Time: 5 mins

Serves: 8

Ingredients:

- 2 ½ cups all-purpose flour
- 4 tsp baking powder
- 1 tsp baking soda
- ½ tsp sea salt
- ½ tsp cinnamon
- ½ cup granulated sugar
- ¼ cup cocoa powder, optional for chocolate pancake mix

Instructions:

1. Mix the ingredients in a bowl until well combined. Store the pancake mix in an airtight container.
2. Use for your pancake recipes.

8. French Onion Soup

Don't feel bad when your onions seem to be softening too quickly. Peel them and make cheesy French onion soup with them.

Prep Time: 20 mins

Cook Time: 1 hour 17 mins

Serves: 4

Ingredients:

- 3 tbsp unsalted butter
- 1 tbsp extra virgin olive oil
- 3 lb. yellow onions (going bad), cleaned and thinly sliced
- 2 cloves garlic, minced
- 2 tbsp all-purpose flour
- ½ cup dry white wine
- 6 cups beef broth or stock, low-sodium
- 4 sprigs fresh thyme or 1 tsp dried thyme
- 2 bay leaves
- Kosher salt and black pepper to taste
- 8 slices baguette
- 2 oz Gruyere cheese, shredded

Instructions:

1. Heat the butter and oil in a medium saucepan over low-medium heat. Sauté the onions for 25 to 30 minutes or until very soft and caramelized. Stir in the garlic and flour, and cook for 1 minute.

2. Pour in the wine and let it cook for 1 to 2 minutes, stir and scrape off any stuck bits at the bottom of the pan.

3. Add the stock, thyme, bay leaves, salt, and black pepper. Bring to a boil over medium heat and then simmer uncovered over low heat for 30 minutes, stirring occasionally.

4. Preheat the oven to 400°F.

5. Place the baguette slices on a baking sheet and toast in the oven for 5 to 6 minutes or until golden brown around the edges.

6. Preheat the broiler to 425°F.

7. Place 4 oven-safe bowls on a large rimmed baking sheet. Spoon the soup into the bowls a little over halfway. Place 2 toasted baguette on each soup and divide the cheese on top. Broil for 2 to 4 minutes or until the cheese melts and lightly browns.

8. Garnish with thyme and serve warm.

9. Thai Peanut Dressing

Now, stuck peanut butter in its container no longer has to go wasted. Give the container a good hot water rinse and use the mixture for Thai peanut dressing or African peanut soup.

Prep Time: 20 mins

Serves: 4

Ingredients:

- 1 to 2 tbsp hot water
- 1 container of stuck bits of creamy peanut butter
- About ¼ cup of creamy peanut butter (from a new container)
- 2 tbsp rice vinegar
- 2 tbsp fresh lime juice
- 2 tbsp low-sodium soy sauce or tamari
- 1 tsp toasted sesame oil
- 1 tbsp honey, maple syrup, or agave nectar
- 1 tsp sriracha
- ¼ tsp ginger paste
- ¼ tsp garlic paste

Instructions:

1. Add hot water to the nearly empty container of peanut butter. Cover and shake vigorously until the stuck peanut butter releases into the liquid; as much of it as you can. Pour the mixture into a bowl.
2. Add the ¼ cup of creamy peanut butter and remaining ingredients. Mix until smooth.
3. Pour the dressing into a serving bowl. Use as desired.

10. Seasoned Crust Mix for Fish and Chicken

Once your bread starts going stale, then it's time for a delicious crusted chicken or fish dish. See how to make a tasty crust mix for that.

Prep Time: 15 mins

Cook Time: 7 mins

Makes: 1 to 2 cups

Ingredients:

- 1 to 2 cups stale bread, cut into cubes
- 1 to 2 tbsp melted butter
- Chicken or fish herb or seasoning mix of choice, to taste

Instructions:

1. Preheat the oven to 400°F.
2. Spread the bread on a baking sheet and toast in the oven for 5 to 7 minutes, mixing halfway.
3. Transfer the bread, butter, and herb or seasoning mix to a food processor. Blitz a couple of times or until ground to your desired texture.
4. Use the crust mix for topping or coating chicken and fish. Adjust the seasoning mix for use with other protein options like lamb, beef, etc.

11. Chocolate Dessert Sauce

Got that last bit of chocolate drink mix lurking in your pantry and not sure what to do with it? Make an easy chocolate sauce for your desserts.

Prep Time: 5 mins

Cook Time: 5 mins

Serves: 8

Ingredients:

- ½ cup heavy cream
- 1 ½ cups instant chocolate drink mix
- ⅛ tsp kosher salt
- 1 ½ tsp vanilla extract

Instructions:

1. Combine the heavy cream, chocolate drink mix, and salt in a small saucepan. Cook over medium heat while stirring until the drink mix dissolves.
2. Let come to a boil while stirring constantly. Then, reduce the heat to low and simmer for 30 seconds. Let cool and stir in the vanilla.
3. Use as desired and refrigerate any extras.

12. Creamy White Chocolate Mocha

Mix leftover brewed or instant coffee and chocolate drink mix and/or cocoa powder in a cup for a delicious mocha drink.

Prep Time: 10 mins

Serves: 1

Ingredients:

- 3 tbsp white chocolate sauce
- 1.5 oz leftover brewed coffee, warm
- 1 tsp leftover chocolate drink mix or cocoa powder
- 1 cup milk
- Whipped cream for topping
- White chocolate chips or shavings for topping

Instructions:

1. In a large cup, mix the white chocolate syrup, coffee, and chocolate drink mix or cocoa powder until smooth. Add the milk and stir.
2. Top with whipped cream and white chocolate chips or shavings.

13. Cookies and Cream Milkshake

Leftover or flattening cookies like Oreos make for a yummy milkshake. Don't sweat their going wasted anymore.

Prep Time: 5 mins

Serves: 1

Ingredients:

- ¼ cup leftover or flattening Oreo cookies, crumbled
- ½ cup milk
- 1 ½ cups vanilla ice cream
- Whipped cream for topping

Instructions:

1. Blitz the Oreo cookies and milk in a blender until mostly smooth. Add the vanilla ice cream and blend until combined.
2. Pour the milkshake into a glass, top with whipped cream, and serve.

14. Popcorn Chocolate Bars

Revamp leftover popcorn with some chocolate support. Here, chocolate bars come to the rescue.

Prep Time: 10 mins

Cook Time: 5 mins

Chill Time: 1 to 2 hours

Serves: 12

Ingredients:

- ⅓ cup chopped dark chocolate or chips
- ½ cup + 1 tbsp milk chocolate
- ¼ cup leftover popcorn
- ¼ cup marshmallows, quartered

Instructions:

1. Line an 8-inch cookie sheet with baking paper leaving a 1-inch overhang on the sides.
2. Melt the chocolate in a double boiler, stir until fully smooth. Let the chocolate cool to room temperature.
3. Combine the popcorn and marshmallow with the cooled chocolate. Evenly spread the mixture on the cookie sheet. Refrigerate for 1 to 2 hours or until set.
4. Break up the chocolate-popcorn and enjoy!

15. Chocolate Bark

Gather all your leftover confectioneries like funfetti sprinkles, pretzels, candied nuts, etc. and make a super decadent chocolate bark from them.

Prep Time: 10 mins

Cook Time: 5 mins

Chill Time: 1 to 2 hours

Serves: 12

Ingredients:

- ⅓ cup chopped dark chocolate or chips
- ½ cup + 1 tbsp milk chocolate
- ¼ to ½ cup leftover confectioneries (funfetti sprinkles, pretzels, dried fruits, candied nuts, crushed candies, etc.)

Instructions:

1. Line an 8-inch cookie sheet with baking paper leaving a 1-inch overhang on the sides.
2. Melt the chocolate in a double boiler, stir until fully smooth. Let the chocolate cool to room temperature.
3. Evenly spread the chocolate on the cookie sheet and sprinkle on the confectioneries. Refrigerate for 1 to 2 hours or until set.
4. Break up the chocolate bark and enjoy!

Refrigerator Leftovers

16. Mixed Fruit Smoothies

Blend overripe fruits into smoothies. Throw in wilting greens for a green smoothie.

Prep Time: 5 mins

Serves: 2

Ingredients:

- 1 cup overripe berries (works for our fruits too)
- ½ cup milk
- 1 tbsp maple syrup or honey
- ½ tsp vanilla extract, optional
- A handful of wilting greens, if preferred

Instructions:

1. Blend the ingredients in a blender until smooth.
2. Pour the smoothie into a glass and enjoy!

17. Herby Yogurt Dressing

Transform old yogurt into a delicious dressing by simply adding some herbs, olive oil, and vinegar.

Prep Time: 10 mins

Serves: 4

Ingredients:

- ¾ cup old yogurt (not spoiled)
- 2 tbsp olive oil
- 2 tbsp rice vinegar
- ½ cup chopped fresh parsley
- ½ cup chopped fresh chives
- 1 small garlic clove, finely minced or pressed
- Kosher salt and black pepper to taste

Instructions:

1. Mix all the ingredients in a bowl. Serve with a salad.

18. Egg Fried Rice

Just a gentle reminder that fried rice prefers leftover cooked rice. Add whatever fresh or frozen soft veggies left from your stash, and throw in some eggs for added protein.

Prep Time: 30 mins

Cook Time: 12 mins

Serves: 4

Ingredients:

- 3 tbsp vegetable oil, divided
- 2 large eggs, whisked
- 1 ½ cups leftover diced veggies (like carrots, onions, bell peppers - fresh or frozen)
- ½ cup frozen peas
- 3 cloves garlic, minced
- Kosher salt and black pepper to taste
- 4 cups cooked leftover rice
- 3 green onions, thinly sliced
- 3 to 4 tbsp soy sauce or to taste
- 2 tsp oyster sauce, optional
- ½ tsp toasted sesame oil

Instructions:

1. Heat 1 tbsp of olive oil in a wok or large skillet over medium heat. Next, add the eggs and scramble them for 2 to 3 minutes or until they are set. Remove them onto a plate.
2. Heat another tbsp of oil in the pan and sauté the vegetables for 3 minutes. Add the peas, cook for 2 minutes, and then cook in the garlic for 1 minute or until fragrant. Spoon the veggies onto a plate.
3. Heat the last bit of oil in the skillet and add the rice and green onions. Stir-fry both until well-heated through, breaking the rice lumps as you mix.
4. Mix the soy sauce, oyster sauce (if using), and sesame oil in a bowl. Drizzle the mixture over the rice and mix until each rice grain is coated with the sauce.
5. Return the eggs and veggies to the pan and mix everything well. Serve warm.

19. Simple Cheese Quesadillas

A quick snack is up your alley using leftover tortillas and melting cheese. Vamp up your serving with fresh tomato or mango salsa.

Prep Time: 5 mins

Cook Time: 3 mins

Serves: 4

Ingredients:

- 2 tortillas (whatever size you have)
- Leftover cheese, grated - melting cheese ideally
- Tomato or mango salsa for serving, optional

Instructions:

1. Grease a skillet with cooking spray and place over low-medium heat.
2. Place one tortilla in the skillet and sprinkle the cheese over it. Cover with the other tortilla and cook for 1 minute. Flip the quesadilla and cook the other side for 1 to 2 minutes or until the cheese melts.
3. Slide the quesadilla onto a cutting board and use a knife to cut it into four wedges.
4. Serve the quesadillas with tomato or mango salsa.

20. Winter Warmer Soup

Add leftover roasted chicken and vegetables to a sizzling pot of broth or stock for a soup that is great to challenge the cold weather.

Prep Time: 10 mins

Cook Time: 36 mins

Serves: 4

Ingredients:

- 2 tbsp olive oil
- 2 to 4 cups of leftover veggies of choice (like carrots, onion, parsnips, leeks, etc.)
- 4 cloves garlic, finely chopped
- 4 cups chicken broth, low-sodium
- 1 cup water
- 2 sprigs fresh tarragon
- 2 sprigs fresh thyme
- 1 bay leaf
- 1 to 2 cups shredded leftover chicken
- Kosher salt and black pepper to taste
- 1 bunch fresh, flat-leaf parsley leaves for garnish

Instructions:

1. Heat the olive oil in a large pot over medium heat. Sauté the vegetables for 5 to 10 minutes or until tender. Stir in the garlic and cook for 1 minute or until fragrant.
2. Add the stock, water, herbs, chicken, salt, and black pepper. Bring to a boil, cover, and simmer for 20 to 25 minutes or until veggies are softer and the chicken heated through. Fish out and discard the herbs. Adjust the taste with salt and black pepper.
3. Garnish with parsley and serve warm.

21. Meat Pasta Casserole

You can simply upgrade cooked leftover pasta with some meat, sauce, and cheese. Serve it for dinner and no one would know.

Prep Time: 10 mins

Cook Time: 22 mins

Serves: 4

Ingredients:

- 1 lb. lean ground beef
- ½ medium onion, chopped
- 1 clove garlic, minced
- Kosher salt and black pepper to taste
- 1 ½ cups marinara sauce
- 2 cups leftover cooked pasta
- 1 cup shredded mozzarella cheese
- ½ cup grated Parmesan cheese

Instructions:

1. Preheat the oven to 400°F.
2. Cook the beef, onion, and garlic in a large pot over medium heat for 7 to 10 minutes or until the beef browns, stirring occasionally and breaking the lumps that form with your spoon. Season with salt and black pepper.
3. Stir through the marinara sauce and pasta. Transfer everything to a casserole dish. Sprinkle on the mozzarella and Parmesan cheeses.
4. Bake uncovered for 10 minutes or until the cheeses melt. Broil further for 1 to 2 minutes to brown the cheese a bit.
5. Rest for 5 minutes before serving.

22. Rice Cakes

Give yourself an Asian snack treat by molding and crisping up some rice cakes from leftover cooked rice. Enjoy it with sweet soy sauce for dipping.

Prep Time: 20 mins

Cook Time: 20 mins

Serves: 8

Ingredients:

For the rice cakes:

- 2 cups cooked leftover rice
- 2 tbsp all-purpose flour
- 1 tbsp vegetable oil
- 1 tbsp sliced chives, optional garnish

For the dipping sauce:

- 1 tbsp granulated sugar
- 1 tbsp soy sauce

Instructions:

For the rice cakes:

1. In a bowl, mix the rice with flour until properly combined. Mold the rice mixture into 6 to 8 patties.
2. Heat the oil in a nonstick skillet over medium heat. Fry the rice cakes for 1 to 2 minutes per side or until light golden brown. Increase the heat to high and fry for 3 to 4 minutes per side or until they attain a deeper golden color and are crispy.
3. Transfer them to a plate and garnish with chives.

For the dipping sauce:

1. Mix the sugar and soy sauce in a bowl.
2. Serve with the rice cakes.

23. Chicken Noodle Soup

Simply no-brainer! Throw leftover cooked chicken, vegetables, and noodles into a pot of boiling broth for that classic soup that drives the flu away.

Prep Time: 10 mins

Cook Time: 32 mins

Serves: 4

Ingredients:

- 1 tbsp butter
- ½ cup chopped onion
- ½ cup chopped celery
- ½ cup diced carrots
- 4 (14.5 oz) cans chicken broth
- 1 (14.5 oz) can vegetable broth
- 1 cup cooked leftover chicken, shredded
- ½ tsp dried basil
- ½ tsp dried oregano
- Kosher salt and black pepper to taste
- 1 cup cooked leftover egg noodles or other noodles that you have
- Chopped fresh parsley for garnish

Instructions:

1. Melt the butter in a large pot over medium heat. Sauté the onion, celery, and carrots for 5 minutes or until tender.
2. Add the broth, chicken, herbs, salt, and black pepper. Bring to a boil, cover, and simmer for 15 to 20 minutes or until the veggies are softer and the chicken heated through.
3. Stir the noodles through and let warm through for 5 to 6 minutes. Adjust the taste with salt and black pepper.
4. Garnish with parsley and serve warm.

24. Garlic Butter Greens

Wilting greens? They are welcome. Sauté them in garlic butter and there you have an effortless side dish.

Prep Time: 10 mins

Cook Time: 7 mins

Serves: 4

Ingredients:

- 1 tbsp butter
- 2 garlic cloves, minced
- 1 to 2 cups wilting greens (kale, spinach, green beans, etc.)
- 2 tbsp vegetable broth, for harder wilting greens

Instructions:

1. Melt the butter in a skillet over medium heat. Sauté the garlic for 1 minute or until fragrant.
2. Add the greens and sauté for 2 to 3 minutes or until fully wilted.
3. To aid harder greens get tender, pour in vegetable broth and cook for 2 to 3 more minutes. Serve right away.

25. Fish Cakes

Leftover cooked potatoes from the other day can simply be transformed into fish cakes. Also, add any extras of canned or cooked fish for a complete job.

Prep Time: 20 mins

Cook Time: 6 mins

Serves: 4

Ingredients:

- 2 cups remaining canned fish (drained) or leftover cooked fish (deboned)
- 1 cup cooked leftover potatoes, broken into small pieces
- ¾ cup panko breadcrumbs
- 2 eggs
- ¼ cup thinly sliced green onion
- 1 tbsp lemon juice
- ½ tbsp Old Bay
- Kosher salt and black pepper to taste
- 2 to 3 tbsp olive oil

Instructions:

1. Combine all the ingredients in a bowl except the oil. Mix well and form into 4 patties. Place on a plate, cover, and refrigerate for 30 minutes.
2. Heat the olive oil in a skillet over medium heat and fry the fish patties for 2 to 3 minutes per side or until golden brown and compacted. Drain on paper towels.
3. Serve with your preferred sauce and salad.

26. Shredded Beef Tacos

When you have leftover steak or other meat types, do think of tacos. They are such a splurge for this zero-waste agenda.

Prep Time: 10 mins

Cook Time: 7 mins

Serves: 4

Ingredients:

- 1 tbsp olive oil
- 1 small white onion, diced
- 2 cups of cooked leftover beef, shredded
- 1 tsp taco seasoning
- Flour tortillas, taco-size for serving
- **Optional toppings:**
- Shredded lettuce
- Salsa
- Guacamole
- Shredded cheddar or Monterey Jack cheese
- Fresh cilantro leaves
- Lime wedges

Instructions:

1. Heat the olive oil in a skillet over medium heat. Sauté the onion for 3 minutes or until tender. Add the beef and taco seasoning; stir-fry for 3 to 4 minutes or until the beef warms through.
2. Serve the beef in the tortillas with your preferred toppings.

27. Chili-Infused Oil

It's great to have chili oil on hand for a quick heat drizzle over foods. You can make one easily from an excess of chilies in your fridge.

Prep Time: 30 mins

Cook Time: 60 mins

Serves: 4

Ingredients:

- 1 ½ cups olive oil
- 6 to 8 chilies

Instructions:

1. Sterilize 1 to 2 small glass bottles.
2. Add the oil and chillies to a small saucepan. Place over medium heat and let it gently heat until you see several tiny bubbles. Next, turn the heat off and let it cool completely.
3. Strain the oil into the bottles and add the chilies to your heat tolerable taste - more chili means spicier oil over time. Cover and keep in a cool, dark, dry place (not the fridge).

28. Rice Pudding

Leftover rice is delicious in rice pudding. All that creaminess and spice is so satisfying.

Prep Time: 10 mins

Cook Time: 10 mins

Serves: 4

Ingredients:

- 1 cup cooked leftover rice
- 1 cup milk
- 1 cup unsweetened condensed milk
- ⅓ cup white sugar
- ¼ tsp salt
- ¼ tsp ground cinnamon or to taste
- 1 tbsp butter
- ½ tsp vanilla extract
- ⅔ cup golden raisins

Instructions:

1. Combine the rice and milk in a saucepan. Cook over medium heat until the rice is a little more tender to your desire and heated through. Take off the heat.
2. Stir in the condensed milk, sugar, cinnamon, butter, and vanilla. Stir the raisins through.
3. Serve warm.

29. Banana Muffins

If you didn't know, overripe bananas are better for banana muffins than regular ripened ones. Overripe bananas give better flavor to these muffins. So don't be worried about overripening bananas again, just make banana muffins with them.

Prep Time: 15 mins

Cook Time: 30 mins

Serves: 12

Ingredients:

- 1 ½ cups all-purpose flour
- 1 tsp baking powder
- 1 tsp baking soda
- ½ tsp salt
- 3 large overripe bananas, peeled and mashed
- ¾ cup granulated sugar
- 1 large egg
- ⅓ cup butter, melted

Instructions:

1. Preheat the oven to 350°F. Grease a 12-cup muffin tin with cooking spray or melted butter.
2. Mix the flour, baking powder and soda, and salt in a bowl. In another bowl, whisk the bananas, egg, sugar, and melted butter. Add the flour mixture and mix until smooth batter forms.
3. Divide the batter between the muffin tin cups, about two-third way up.
4. Bake for 25 to 30 minutes or until baked through. Rest the muffins in the tin for 5 minutes then transfer them to a wire rack to cool completely. Enjoy!

30. Cake Crumb Pie Crust

Cake crumb crust tastes amazing in pies, tarts, etc. Use stale cake crumbs to create one.

Prep Time: 10 mins

Cook Time: 15 mins

Makes: 1 pie crust

Ingredients:

- 3 cups cake crumbs
- 1 cup butter

Instructions:

1. Preheat the oven to 350°F.
2. Add the cake crumbs and butter to a bowl. Knead until well combined. Press the mixture into the bottom and sides of an increased pie pan.
3. Bake for 10 to 15 minutes or until golden. Cool completely. Keep refrigerated until ready to use for your pie recipe.

Conclusion

Happy to join the zero food waste wagon?

We're excited to support you on this journey. No longer should little bits of food leftovers become a burden. With the recipes shared, making good use of the food you've got, reducing cost, and becoming more sustainable becomes an easy feat.

We hope you enjoyed each recipe and would gradually give them a try while you create your unique versions too.

Dear Reader

First and foremost, I would like to express my gratitude for downloading and reading my book. I hope that you found it informative and enjoyable. Writing books is my way of sharing my skills and expertise with readers like you.

I am aware that there are countless books available, and I am truly grateful that you chose mine. Your decision means a lot to me, and I am confident that you made the right choice.

If you could provide me with honest feedback about my book, it would make me even happier. Feedback is essential for growth and development. It helps me to improve the content of my book and generate new ideas for future publications. Who knows, your feedback might just spark an idea for my next book!

Thank you once again for taking the time to read my book, and I hope to hear from you soon.

Sincerely,

Martin Beasant

Printed in Dunstable, United Kingdom